KOLBY AND HIS FRIENDS START THE C B I. THE CBI PLEDGES TO TEACH FINANCIAL RESPONSIBILTY TO INCREASE GENERATIONAL WEALTH

THROUGH HOME-OWNERSHIP, RESPONSIBLE BANKING PRACTICES, AND SAFE INVESTMENTS

CHECKING ACCOUNTS ACCEPTS DEPOSITS AND ALLOW WITHDRAWALS. YOU ALSO GET A DEBIT CARD SO YOU CAN ACCESS YOUR MONEY WHEN YOU TRAVEL. PAY FOR A HOTEL OR EAT AT A RESTAURANT.

A LENDER MANAGES YOUR ACCOUNTS AND HELPS WHEN YOU NEED A LOAN... LIKE BUYING A HOME! THEY ALSO SHOW YOU HOW TO SAVE MONEY TO INCREASE YOUR PERSONAL WEALTH! LET'S LOOK AT TWO WAYS TO SAVE: CERTIFICATES OF DEPOSITS AND SAVINGS ACCOUNTS.

THE CBI EXPLAINS HOW MONEY EARNS INTEREST

PARKER IS A DEPUTY WITH THE CBI. HE TAKES HIS MONEY TO THE BANK. THE TOTAL IS $100.00 HE CONTINUES TO DEPOSIT $5.00 EACH MONTH FOR 36 MONTHS. $5.00 X 36 = $180.00
THE BANK PAYS .50 AS A YEARLY INTEREST CALLED THE APY (ANNUAL PERCENTAGE YIELD). HE EARNS $2.82 OR .94 A YEAR.

LAYLA DOESN'T THINK THAT'S MUCH, BUT PARKER REMINDS HER HE IS VERY YOUNG, SO HE HAS LOTS OF TIME TO SAVE AND INVEST AND ONE DAY HE'LL HAVE A LOT OF MONEY.
TOTAL SAVINGS BREAKDOWN:

INTEREST EARNED	$2.82
TOTAL CONTRIBUTIONS	+ $180
INITIAL DEPOSIT	+ $100
YOUR TOTAL SAVING	$282.82

A CD WORKS THE SAME WAY, EXCEPT WHEN YOU DEPOSIT MONEY IT IS SECURED FOR A TERM OF 12 MONTHS, 18 MONTHS, OR 24 MONTHS. (IF YOU TAKE IT OUT EARLY, WE WILL PENALIZE YOU. THIS MEANS YOU WILL LOSE SOME OF THE INTEREST EARNED, BUT NEVER THE PRINCIPAL)
IT CAN ALSO BE CALLED AN IRA (INDIVIDUAL RETIREMENT ACCOUNT)

HE ASKS LAYLA, HOW MUCH MONEY HAS SHE SAVED... SHE SAYS "NONE".
PARKER REMINDS HER THAT LEARNING HOW TO SAVE IS ONE WAY TO IMPACT GENERATIONAL POVERTY; THERE ARE OTHER WAYS TO SAVE AND INVEST, BUT WE'LL JUST EXPLORE A FEW FOR NOW.

[Y]DEN AND DALLAS ARE CREDIT DEPUTIES. THEY ARE [R]ESPONSIBLE FOR REMINDING PEOPLE TO MONITOR [T]HEIR CREDIT FOR INACCURACIES AND CARRYING TOO [M]UCH DEPT! THE CREDIT DEPUTIES AND THE CBI EXPLAIN THE DIFFERENCE BETWEEN CREDIT SCORES AND CREDIT HISTORY THIS WAY:
[C]REDIT REPORTS AND CREDIT SCORES ARE TWO DIFFERENT THINGS. A CREDIT REPORT IS A STATEMENT [TH]AT HAS INFORMATION ABOUT YOUR CREDIT ACTIVITY AND CURRENT CREDIT SITUATION SUCH AS PAYING, [L]OAN HISTORY AND THE STATUS OF YOUR CREDIT AC[C]OUNTS. YOUR CREDIT SCORES ARE BASED ON THE INFORMATION IN YOUR CREDIT REPORT.
WWW.CONSUMERFINANCE.GOV

YOUR CREDIT HISTORY AND BEHAVIOR FORM THE BASIS OF YOUR CREDIT SCORE

- PAYMENT HISTORY
- CURRENT UNPAID DEPT
- LENGTH OF CREDIT HISTORY
- % OF AVAILABLE CREDIT USED
- TYPE OF DEPT AND WHEN IT STARTED
- NEW APPLICATIONS FOR CREDIT

TOO MUCH DEPT IS A BURDEN AND CAN PREVENT YOU FROM BUYING A HOUSE OR GETTING A LOAN WHEN YOU REALLY NEED ONE. IN OTHER WORDS PAY YOUR CREDIT CARDS OFF EACH MONTH AND THAT WILL INCREASE YOUR CAPACITY.

KOLBY SAYS TO THINK OF CAPACITY LIKE BREATHING. IF YOU SMOKE CIGARETTES, IT WILL LIMIT YOUR LUNG CAPACITY GIVING YOU LESS OXYGEN AVAILABLE FOR BREATHING. IF YOU OWE A LOT OF MONEY ON YOUR CREDIT CARD, YOU'LL HAVE LESS AVAILABLE TO USE WHEN YOU NEED IT. LENDERS VIEW THIS AS POOR MONEY MANAGEMENT AND RISKY BEHAVIOR.

DREW AND KAYLEN WILL WRITE YOU A TICKET IF YOU DON'T PAY YOUR DEBTS ON TIME. BUT FIRST, THEY'LL SEND YOU A CREDIT ALERT. CREDIT CARD COMPANIES SEND WARNINGS WHEN A CHANGE HAPPENS TO YOUR CREDIT FILE. AN EXAMPLE IS WHEN A LENDER REQUESTS YOUR CREDIT. THIS IS IMPORTANT ESPECIALLY IF SOMEONE IS PRETENDING TO BE YOU TO OBTAIN CREDIT IN THEIR NAME. THIS IS FRAUD!

OME HOMEBUYERS IN THE COMMUNITY ARE ANXIOUS. THEY WORRY THEY HAVEN'T SAVED ENOUGH OR MANAGED THEIR DEBT PROPERLY. THEY EPORT BAD EXPERIENCES WITH UNTRUSTWORTHY SALESPERSONS. THE J RECOMMENDS THEY KNOW THE LAW BEFORE SIGNING ANY DOCUMENTS ND REFERS THEM TO THE DEPT OF HOUSING AND URBAN DEVELOPMENT OR MORE COMMONLY CALLED "HUD". THE COMMUNITY SAYS THEY'VE NEVER HEARD OF HUD... ARE THEY IN OUR NEIGHBORHOOD?

THE CBI IS EXCITED THE COMMUNITY WANTS TO KNOW MORE ABOUT HU
LAYLA SAYS. "I'LL TAKE THIS ONE! 'THERE ARE HUD OFFICES ACROSS
THE COUNTRY. "SOME LENDERS ARE ALSO HUD COUNSELORS. 'THIS
MEANS THEY ARE INFORMED ABOUT FAIR HOUSING RULES. 'THEY HOLD
SPECIAL CERTIFICATE THAT SAYS THEY HAVE PASSED STRINGENT TEST
REQUIRED BY THE GOVERNMENT."
MORTAGE LENDERS ARE IDENTIFIED BY A GROUP OF NUMBERS FROM TH
NMLS NATION-WIDE MORTGAGE LICENSING SYSTEM

ND ANOTHER THING, LET'S MAKE SURE YOU KNOW HOW TO CHECK YOUR CREDIT CORE IT'S FREE AND SPONSORED BY THE THREE CREDIT REPORTING BUREAUS: QUIFAX, EXPERIAN, AND TRANS UNION. BUT THE EASIEST WAY TO GET ALL THREE IS TO GO TO WWW.ANNUALCREDITREPORT.COM.

KOLBY SUGGESTS THEY ATTEND A HOME BUYING SEMINAR. HE SAYS, "KNOW BEFORE YOU GO".

HOMEBUYING WORKSHOP IS SPONSORED BY QUALIFIED PROFESSIONALS WHO DELIVER INFORMATION REGARDING PURCHASING, MAINTENANCE, AND PROTECTION FOR BOTH RENTERS AND HOMEOWNERS.
A WORKSHOP, YOU MAY FIND REALTORS, LENDERS, APPRAISERS INSPECTORS, INSURANCE AGENTS, BUILDERS, ATTORNEYS, HUD COUNSELORS, AND OTHER INTERESTED PARTIES.

 LOCATION WHERE YOU BUY.

 CONDITION: IS THE HOUSE IN GOOD SHAPE?

 NEIGHBORHOOD: HOW GOOD ARE THE SCHOOLS IN YOUR NEIGHBORHOOD?

 IMPROVEMENTS: DID YOU REPLACE THE ROOF?

 MARKET: ARE THERE PE[OPLE] BUYING HOUSES?

THERE ARE AT LEAST FIVE THINGS THAT IMPACT THE EQUITY [IN] YOUR HOUSE.

HEN YOU RENT, YOU MAY AS WELL THROW MONEY OUT THE WINDOW BECAUSE YOUR MENTS DO NOT BUILD EQUITY. REMEMBER, YOU DO NOT OWN THE HOME! BUT WHEN YOU BUY A HOUSE, YOUR PAYMENTS CONTRIBUTE TO CREATING EQUITY FOR YOUR AMILY. HOUSES APPRECIATE IN VALUE WHEN WE MAINTAIN OUR PROPERTY. MOWING GRASS, PAINTING, AND REPAIRING THE ROOF, ARE ALL WAYS TO ADD VALUE TO YOUR HOME.

KOLBY AND THE CBI PROMISE TO HELP EVERYONE BECOME
HOMEOWNER. NOW THE HARD PART; PRACTICE WHAT YOU'V
LEARNED.
ONLY SHOP FOR WHAT YOU NEED. CLIP COUPONS OR BUY I
BULK WHEN POSSIBLE.

ARTER FOR SERVICES, INSTEAD OF PAYING CASH. LET'S SAY YOUR NEIGHBOR IS A CARPENTER AND YOU ARE AN ACCOUNTANT. SHE NEEDS SOMEONE TO DO HER AXES, AND YOU NEED SOMEONE TO BUILD YOUR FENCE, BARTER! ONE GOOD DEED FOR ANOTHER! TAKE YOUR LUNCH TO WORK, MAKE YOUR OWN COFFEE

BE LIKE A THRIFTY BIRD AND BUILD A NEST EGG OF HARDWORK AND COOL CASH.
MAINTAIN YOUR PROPERTY AND BE A GOOD NEIGHBOR. PAY YOUR BILLS ON TIME AND STICK TO YOUR BUDGET.

KOLBY AND CBI WANT YOU TO KICK POVERTY OUT! AND DON'T FORGET, KOLBY AND CBI IS ALWAYS READY TO HELP!

www.ingramcontent.com/pod-product-compliance
Lightning Source LLC
Chambersburg PA
CBHW041409160426
42811CB00106B/1563